W9-AYV-409

SIMPLY SCIENCE

Atoms

by Melissa Stewart

Content Adviser: Mats Selen, Ph.D.,
Department of Physics, University of Illinois at Champaign-Urbana

Science Adviser: Terrence E. Young Jr., M.Ed., M.L.S.,
Jefferson Parish (La.) Public Schools

Reading Adviser: Dr. Linda D. Labbo,
Department of Reading Education, College of Education,
The University of Georgia

 COMPASS POINT BOOKS
Minneapolis, Minnesota

Compass Point Books
3109 West 50th Street, #115
Minneapolis, MN 55410

Visit Compass Point Books on the Internet at www.compasspointbooks.com
or e-mail your request to custserv@compasspointbooks.com

Photographs ©: DigitalVision, cover; Steve Strickland/Visuals Unlimited, 4; Wolfe/gtphoto, 5;
Unicorn Stock Photos/Dennis MacDonald, 6; Novastock/The Image Finders, 7; Bob Krist/Corbis,
8; IBMRL/Visuals Unlimited, 10; Picture Press/Corbis, 11; Tom & Therisa Stack/Tom Stack &
Associates, 12 (top left), 28; Richard T. Nowitz, 12 (top right); Spencer Swanger/Tom Stack &
Associates, 12 (bottom left); Ernest H. Rogers, 12 (bottom right); Archivo Iconographico,
S.A./Corbis, 15; Roger Ressmeyer/Corbis, 19; Brand X Pictures, 20; George Disario/Corbis, 23;
Skjold Photographs, 24; Marilyn Moseley LaMantia, 27.

Editors: E. Russell Primm, Emily J. Dolbear, Pam Rosenberg, and Catherine Neitge
Photo Researchers: Svetlana Zhurkina and Marcie Spence
Photo Selector: Linda S. Koutris
Designer/Page Production: Bradfordesign, Inc./Erin Scott, SARIN creative

Library of Congress Cataloging-in-Publication Data
Stewart, Melissa.
Atoms / by Melissa Stewart.
   p. cm. — (Simply science)
Includes bibliographical references and index.
Contents: What is matter?—Matter is made of atoms—Early ideas about atoms—Atoms and
elements—Molecules and compounds—What is a chemical reaction—The importance of atoms.
ISBN 0-7565-0441-4 (hardcover)
   1. Atomic theory—Juvenile literature. 2. Atoms—Juvenile literature. [1. Atoms. 2. Atomic
theory.] I. Title. II. Series: Simply science (Minneapolis, Minn.)
   QD461 .S838 2003
   539.7—dc21   2002015113

© 2003 by Compass Point Books
All rights reserved. No part of this book may be reproduced without written permission from the publisher. The publisher
takes no responsibility for the use of any of the materials or methods described in this book, nor for the products thereof.
Printed in the United States of America.

Table of Contents

*Note: In this book, words that are defined in the glossary are in **bold** the first time they appear in the text.*

What Is Matter?

Close your eyes and picture your bedroom. You probably see a bed, a dresser, and a closet full of clothes. You may also have some toys and books. Maybe you even have a tank full of fish or some balloons full of air. Can you think of anything that a bed, a dresser, clothes, toys, books, fish, and balloons all have in common? All of these things are made up of **matter**.

Everything in this bedroom is made up of matter.

Living things, such as these fish, are made up of matter, too.

Everything in the world is made up of matter. You are made of matter. So are your clothes, your bed, and the sandwich you will eat for lunch. Even the water in a fish tank, the air inside a balloon, and the pages of this book are made up of matter. Matter is anything that takes up space.

Just like everything else in the world, people are made up of matter.

Even the air in these balloons is made up of matter.

Matter Is Made of Atoms

Now imagine a set of building blocks. There are large and small square blocks. Maybe there are rectangular blocks, too. They are all blocks. Now think about what you can build with the blocks. Maybe you want to build a tower. When you finish the tower you might want to take it apart and build a car. You can build anything you want with that same set of blocks. **Atoms** are like those building blocks. They are the tiniest bits of matter. Atoms are so small that you can't see them,

This boy can build many different things with just one set of building blocks.

unless you look through a high-powered **microscope**. More than a billion atoms could fit inside the period at the end of this sentence. All matter is made of atoms.

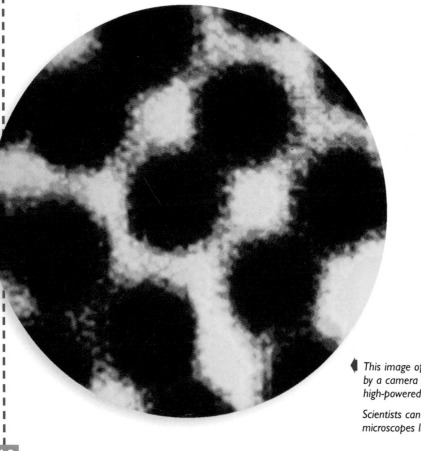

◀ This image of atoms was taken by a camera attached to a high-powered microscope.

Scientists can see atoms with electron ▶ microscopes like this one.

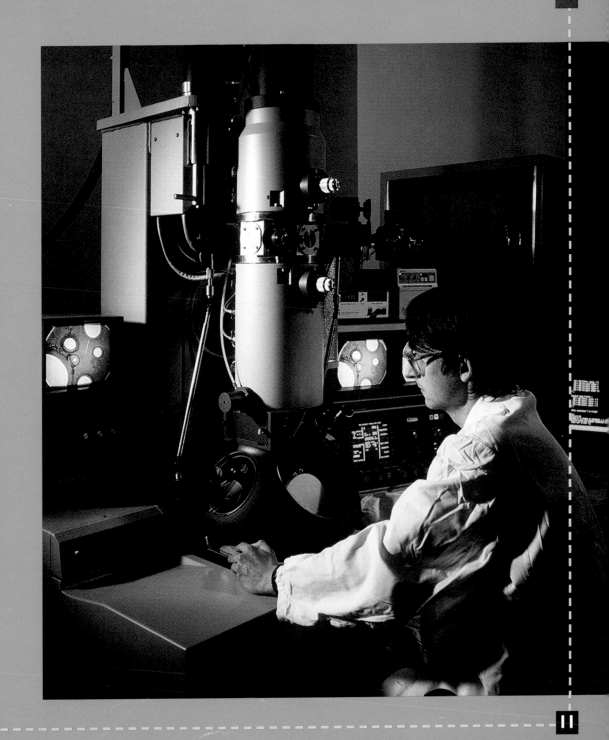

Early Ideas About Atoms

Because atoms are so small, people have not always known about them. The first ideas about atoms came from people living in Greece about 2,400 years ago. People then thought that everything on Earth was made of just four **elements**—earth, wind, fire, and water.

A man named Leucippus had some of the first ideas about atoms. His student, Democritus, became well known for explaining those ideas. These men thought that each element

Long ago, scientists believed everything on Earth was made of earth, wind, fire, and water.

was made up of just one kind of *atomos*. This Greek word means "something that cannot be divided." Democritus said that *atomos* were the smallest bits of matter. They could not be divided into anything else. The ancient Greeks were on the right track, but now we have a better understanding of atoms, elements, and matter. We know that earth, wind, fire, and water are not elements.

Democritus explained the first ideas about atoms. ▶

Periodic Table of the Elements

1 H																	2 He
3 Li	4 Be											5 B	6 C	7 N	8 O	9 F	10 Ne
11 Na	12 Mg											13 Al	14 Si	15 P	16 S	17 Cl	18 Ar
19 K	20 Ca	21 Sc	22 Ti	23 V	24 Cr	25 Mn	26 Fe	27 Co	28 Ni	29 Cu	30 Zn	31 Ga	32 Ge	33 As	34 Se	35 Br	36 Kr
37 Rb	38 Sr	39 Y	40 Zr	41 Nb	42 Mo	43 Tc	44 Ru	45 Rh	46 Pd	47 Ag	48 Cd	49 In	50 Sn	51 Sb	52 Te	53 I	54 Xe
55 Cs	56 Ba	57 La	72 Hf	73 Ta	74 W	75 Re	76 Os	77 Ir	78 Pt	79 Au	80 Hg	81 Tl	82 Pb	83 Bi	84 Po	85 At	86 Rn
87 Fr	88 Ra	89 Ac	104 Rf	105 Db	106 Sg	107 Bh	108 Hs	109 Mt	110 Uun	111 Uuu	112 Uub	113 Uut	114 Uuq		116 Uuh		118 Uuo

58 Ce	59 Pr	60 Nd	61 Pm	62 Sm	63 Eu	64 Gd	65 Tb	66 Dy	67 Ho	68 Er	69 Tm	70 Yb	71 Lu
90 Th	91 Pa	92 U	93 Np	94 Pu	95 Am	96 Cm	97 Bk	98 Cf	99 Es	100 Fm	101 Md	102 No	103 Lr

LEGEND	**Black** ... Solid	Green ... Liquid	**Blue** ... Gas	**Red Outline** ... Synthetically prepared

Atoms and Elements

Today we know that there are about 100 different elements, each one made from its own kind of atoms. These are all shown in a special chart called the **Periodic Table of the Elements**.

Many elements have familiar names, such as gold, oxygen, and iron. Each of these elements is a basic material that cannot be broken down into any simpler materials. The atoms of each element are like building blocks. Each atom of a certain element is exactly like every other atom of that element.

◀ *The Periodic Table of the Elements lists all the known elements.*

Molecules and Compounds

Atoms often combine with other atoms to form **molecules**. If the atoms in a molecule are different from each other, we call the molecule a **compound**. An example of a compound molecule is water. Each water molecule is made from two hydrogen atoms combined with one oxygen atom.

When atoms form molecules, their **properties** may change. For example, when hydrogen atoms combine with other hydrogen atoms, they form molecules of hydrogen gas.

Molecules are formed when atoms join together. ▶

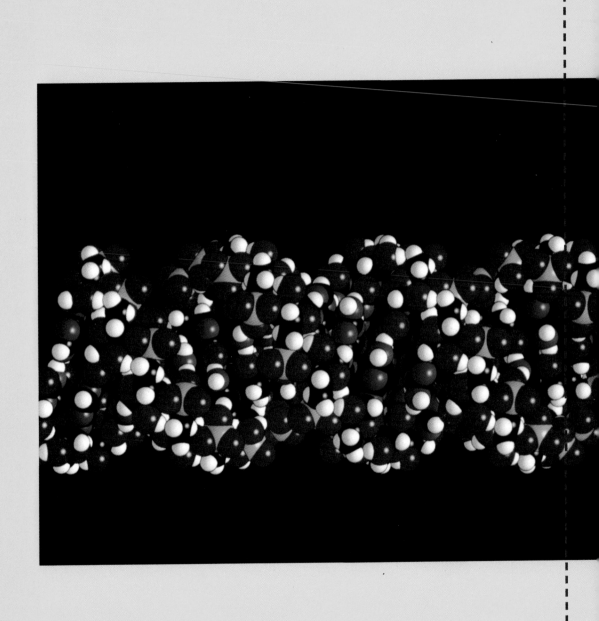

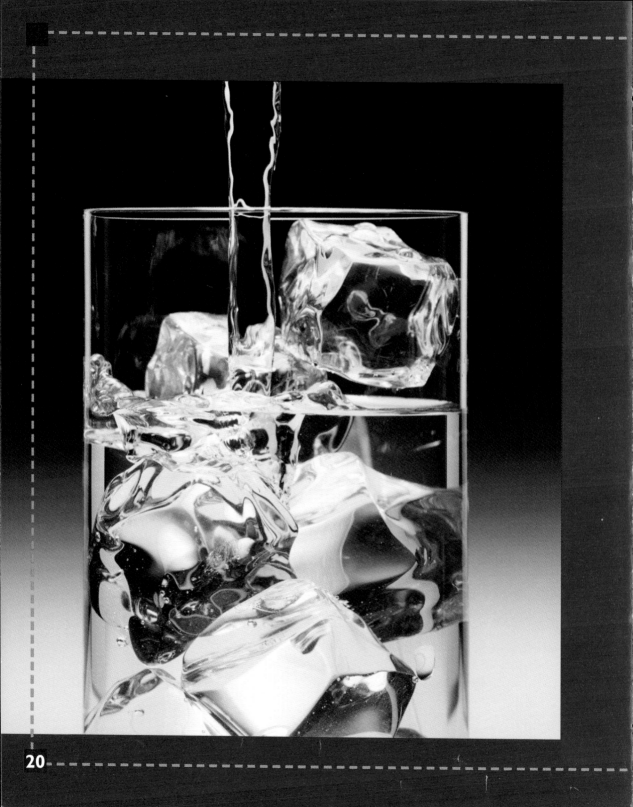

When oxygen atoms combine with other oxygen atoms, they form molecules of oxygen gas. When oxygen atoms combine with hydrogen atoms, however, they can form molecules of water.

◀ *The water in this glass is made up of molecules containing hydrogen and oxygen atoms.*

What Is a Chemical Reaction?

Sometimes when different molecules are mixed together, the atoms will rearrange themselves to form new kinds of molecules. This is called a chemical reaction. If you mix together baking soda and vinegar you will get lots of fizzing and bubbling. This happens because the atoms that make up the molecules of vinegar and the molecules of baking soda are rearranging themselves to make new molecules. The fizzing and bubbling you see when you mix vinegar and baking soda come from a gas called carbon dioxide.

A chemical reaction takes place when baking soda is added to vinegar.

Carbon dioxide is one of the new molecules made in this chemical reaction.

Chemical reactions are happening all around you all the time. They make bread rise, change grape juice into wine, and make a campfire burn. If chemical reactions did not happen inside your body, you would not be able to digest food or flex your muscles. Chemical reactions are what turn the food you eat into bones and muscle and other compounds that are important for you to live.

A chemical reaction will make this bread dough rise.

The Importance of Atoms

Atoms are the building blocks that everything in the world is made of. The air you breathe, the toys you play with, the people you know, are all made of atoms. They make up everything we see, hear, feel, smell, and taste.

You may be wondering if there is anything even smaller than atoms. The answer to this is yes. Atoms are made of even smaller building blocks called particles. The wonderful thing about this is that only three different kinds of particles are needed to explain all

Atoms are made of protons, neutrons, and electrons. ▶

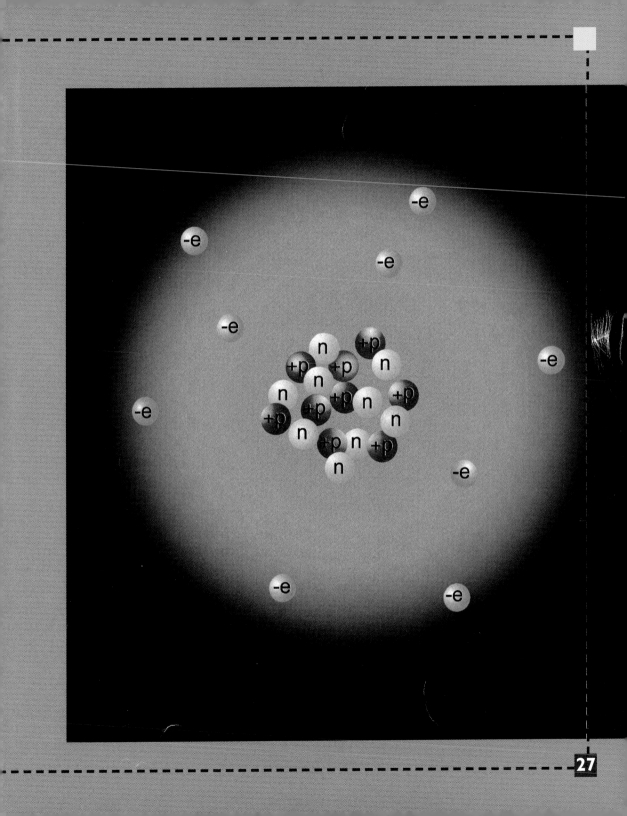

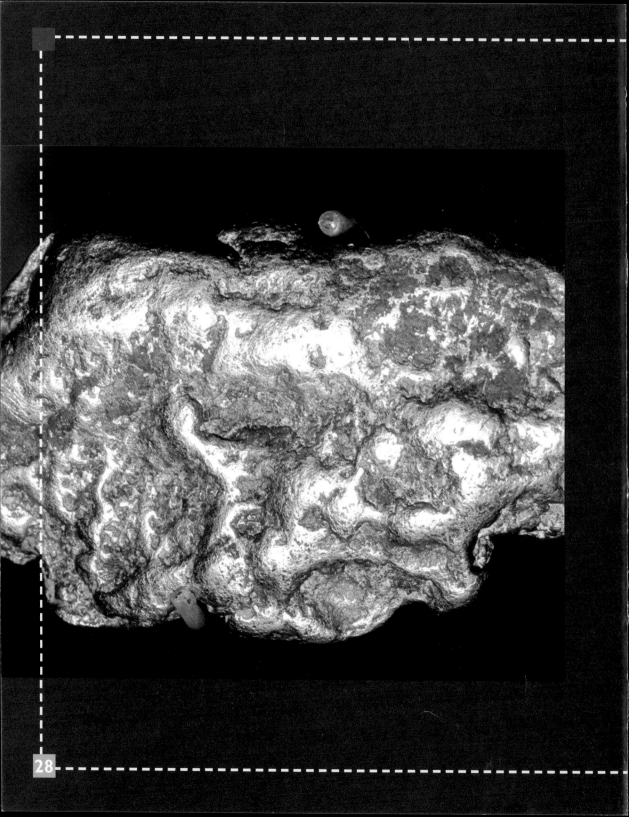

of the 100 or so different kinds of atoms that we know about. These three kinds of particles are called protons, neutrons, and electrons. For example, a helium atom is made up of two protons, two neutrons, and two electrons. A gold atom is made up of 79 protons, 118 neutrons, and 79 electrons. The more we learn about atoms, the more we realize how important and how interesting they are.

◀ The atoms of gold in this gold nugget contain protons, neutrons, and electrons.

Glossary

atom—the smallest piece of an element that still has all the properties of the element

compound—a material made up of two or more kinds of atoms

element—a material that contains only one kind of atom

matter—anything that takes up space as a solid, liquid, or gas

microscope—a device used to see very small objects

molecule—a group of atoms that forms the smallest piece of a material that still has all the properties of the material

Periodic Table of the Elements—a chart that shows all the elements in a way that helps scientists know which ones have similar properties

property—a trait or characteristic that helps make identification possible

Did You Know?

• The protons, neutrons, and electrons that make up an atom are always arranged in the same way. The protons and neutrons are lumped together in the center of an atom. They make up the atom's tiny nucleus. Electrons whiz around the nucleus.

Want to Know More?

At the Library

Cooper, Christopher. *Matter*. New York: DK Publishing, 2000.

Fullick, Ann. *Matter*. Chicago: Heinemann Library, 1999.

Gay, Kathlyn. *Science in Ancient Greece*. Danbury, Conn.: Franklin Watts, 1998.

On the Web

How Things Work

http://howthingswork.virginia.edu/

To ask a science expert questions about atoms, molecules, and matter

The Science Explorer

http://www.exploratorium.edu/science_explorer/index.html

For fun hands-on activities and experiments about all kinds of science subjects

Through the Mail

Smithsonian Institution

P.O. Box 37012

SI Building, Room 153, MRC 010

Washington, DC 20013-7012

To write for more information about the museum's exhibits on atoms and molecules

On the Road

Museum of Science

Science Park

Boston, MA 02114-1099

617/723-2500

To check out exhibits that explore many different areas of science

Index

About the Author

Melissa Stewart earned a bachelor's degree in biology from Union College and a master's degree in science and environmental journalism from New York University. She has written more than thirty books for children and has contributed articles to a variety of magazines for adults and children. In her free time, Melissa enjoys hiking and canoeing near her home in Marlborough, Massachusetts.